LONDON BUSES IN COLOUR: 1960s

Kevin McCormack

Ian Allan
PUBLISHING

First published 2000

ISBN 0 7110 2722 6

© Kevin McCormack 2000

Published by Ian Allan Publishing

an imprint of Ian Allan Publishing Ltd, Terminal House, Shepperton, Surrey TW17 8AS.

Printed by Ian Allan Printing Ltd, Riverdene Business Park, Hersham, Surrey KT12 4RG.

Code: 0006/B2

Classic Design

Front cover: In this scene dating from November 1967, the superbly-proportioned lines of RT1083 are appropriately set against the backdrop of Trafalgar Square's fine stone buildings including, on the right, St Martin-in-the-Fields, dating from 1724. Route 59A was withdrawn in March 1972, being partly covered by Route 159. *Vernon Murphy*

Spider's Web

Back Cover: This intricate overhead wiring marked the junction of trolleybus Routes 601/605 and 604 at Hampton Wick, by the approach to Kingston Bridge. In this view No 1393 had only four weeks to go before the final stage of trolleybus abandonment was implemented on 9 May 1962. *Geoff Rixon*

Underground Overground

Title Page: Encouraged by the reduced maintenance costs, in pre-graffiti days, of having unpainted electric trains, LT ordered one Routemaster, RM664, in bare aluminium. However, the experiment failed due to the vehicle's deteriorating appearance, caused mainly by the effect of garage washing plants. Between July 1961 and December 1962 the 'Silver Lady' operated out of Highgate garage, usually on Route 276, on which duty it was photographed crossing Westminster Bridge on a hazy day. *Trevor Saunders*

On the Starting Grid

Above left: The hub of Green Line services was Victoria where, in Buckingham Palace Road, RT1021 is seen waiting for a rush of motor racing fans in September 1968. A total of 85 RTs carried coach livery and this vehicle was one of the final 16 to be converted in 1960. *Dave Brown*

Introduction

This colour album of London Transport (LT)'s red bus and country bus and coach operations in the 1960s is a companion volume to *London Buses in Colour: 1970s*, published by Ian Allan in October 1999.

In the previous book, we saw how the fledgling NBC subsidiary London Country Bus Services (LCBS) tried to cope with the ailing Country bus and Green Line network inherited from LT on 1 January 1970; also the extent to which both LT and LCBS were plagued by the poor reliability of unsuitable modern vehicles, with reliance being placed on elderly RTs and RFs to help maintain services. The seeds of disarray were, in fact, sown in the 1960s, and stemmed primarily from a belated reaction by LT to modernise its operations in the light of a downturn in passenger traffic.

The 1960s started on an optimistic note. The first production AEC Routemasters — RMs — had just begun to enter service, and were intended to be the mainstay of LT's fleet for years to come. The priority was to use the RMs to replace the ageing trolleybus fleet, a task which was completed by May 1962 — earlier than intended due to the postwar Q1 class being purchased by Spanish operators. RMs would then be employed on replacing the RT family over a predicted 16-year period at the rate of about 350 per year. This would create a fleet of over 7,000 RMs. Yet, in the event, only 2,760 Routemasters were built for LT.

The cause of this shift in policy was LT's growing realisation that the Routemaster's design dated back to the start of the 1950s and the bus

Radioactive

Right: Withdrawn by LT in October 1963, this former Green Line coach was one of 10 subsequently used by British European Airways (BEA) for airside duties, which required the fitting of a radio and flashing roof light. RF273 was photographed at Heathrow in September 1964. *Mike Harries*

was, therefore, virtually obsolete by the time production was in full swing. Other operators were turning to one-person operation (OPO), which required vehicles with an entrance at the front and the engine located elsewhere. LT saw this as the antidote to the declining market and increasing staff shortages. The preferred solution was a new generation of Routemasters, built to the necessary OPO configuration, but using, wherever possible, parts which were interchangeable with conventional RMs. A prototype (FRM1) was constructed, but the project was abandoned for political reasons, and LT was forced to purchase off-the-shelf and largely unproven OPO vehicles instead. LT's problems were exacerbated by deteriorating industrial relations which culminated in a crippling overtime ban in early 1966, causing the suspension of many services, two of which were never reinstated. Nevertheless, confident of the success of OPO and by now fully committed to 100% conversion from crew operation, LT embarked on its Bus Reshaping Plan, heralding the withdrawal of many conductor-operated services and the shortening or rearrangement of numerous routes. So it was that LT had begun the decade as a very traditional bus operator and ended it as one of the most radical.

The 1960s closed with LT's sphere of operations within what had been roughly a 30-mile radius of central London being cut back to the GLC area (the London boroughs) after 36 years (ie since LT's inception). Henceforth, LT would be confined to the red bus network.

In illustrating this book, I have endeavoured to use hitherto unpublished photographs, and am very grateful to the following contributors: Gerald Mead, Dave Brown, Mike Harries (deceased), Roy Hobbs, John Aldridge, Geoff Rixon, Vernon Murphy, Robin Hannay, Trevor Saunders, Hugh Ramsey, John May and Maurice Bateman. For factual information, I have referred, in particular, to Capital Transport's definitive publications *RT — The Story of a London Bus* by Ken Blacker and *London Buses in the 1960s* by Ken Glazier.

Finally, I hope you will enjoy this historical perspective of LT's extensive bus and coach operations and the 1960s atmosphere generated through these pages.

Kevin R. McCormack
Ashtead, Surrey
January 2000

Trial and Error

Left: This view taken in May 1966 at the foot of Highgate Hill depicts Daimler Fleetline XF5, on loan from the Country Area, passing identically-bodied Leyland Atlantean XA40. The buses were participating in comparative trials between the XA, XF and RML classes. The XAs performed the worst due to their more troublesome engines, which was unfortunate as there were 50 XAs, yet only eight XFs. *Maurice Bateman*

Painting the Town Red

Above: A shortage of green RTs at Stevenage garage in the winter of 1965/6 brought several newly-overhauled red RTs to this rapidly-expanding new town. RT1339 pulls away from the bus station in February 1966, shortly before the arrival of further green RTs displaced at High Wycombe by new RMLs. *Maurice Bateman*

Off into the Sunset

Left: 61 years of electric traction in London was coming to an end when this evening shot was taken of trolleybus No 1480 leaving Kingston for its home depot. Route 601 became RM-operated Route 281 on 9 May 1962. *Roy Hobbs*

Contrasting Styles

Above: The sleek lines of the 1938-designed RT bodywork make the postwar standard provincial shape of the low-height RLH type look positively dated. This view was taken at Guildford in April 1969, four years before RLH50 was exported to Auckland, New Zealand. *Dave Brown*

7

Off the Map

Left: Route 84 was one of a handful of red bus services which penetrated deep into the Country Area and terminated beyond the boundaries of the Central Area map. Saunders-bodied roofbox RT4254 stands at the southern terminus at Arnos Grove station in summer 1965. The New Barnet to St Albans section of Route 84 passed to London Country in April 1982. *Dave Brown*

Close Call

Below: The unique rear-engined Routemaster, FRM1, visits Victoria on 29 June 1967, four days after its entry into service. This bus was lucky to survive a fire caused by leaking flywheel oil while in service on 31 August 1967. The absence of opening windows, due to the installation of a forced-air system, resulted in firemen breaking an upstairs window to let the smoke escape. FRM1 re-entered service on 1 December 1967 with opening windows. *Maurice Bateman*

Ups and Downs

Left: Former RT106 was the penultimate prewar RT to remain in stock and was used for training breakdown crews in the art of righting overturned buses. Converted to No 1036TV in 1955, this unhappy vehicle was photographed at Stonebridge Park garage on 7 April 1967. *John Aldridge*

Wrong Numbers

Above: This rare view taken at Chiswick Works on 18 July 1968 depicts AEC Merlins MBS42, MB130 and MBA172. These represent the three basic types — standee, suburban flat-fare and Red Arrow — the latter demonstrating the preferred higher driving position which the first 150 (MBA16-165) lacked. Protracted negotiations with employee representatives over OPO delayed their entry into service such that they were re-registered with G-suffixes. *John Aldridge*

Exposing The Myth

Below: Here is evidence that Green Line vehicles did, after all, carry advertising, albeit discreetly. The coach fleet contained 112 Routemasters; one of the 69 shorter vehicles, RMC1458, speeds across Wisley Common in December 1967. It has been through its first overhaul because the embossed bullseye emblem between the decks has given way to a large transfer. *Mike Harries*

Photocall

Right: Leyland Atlantean XA12 was briefly displayed at Parliament Square on 7 November 1965, the first day of Atlantean operation in London. Chalk Farm's XAs ousted RMs on Route 24 as a prelude to the comparative trials with brand-new RMLs. By this time, the end was nigh for the 8ft-wide RTW class, represented here by RTW437, being pursued by one of the 200 RMs to receive an illuminated offside advertisement display. *John Aldridge*

Going Down the Tubes

Left: For sixty years, Route 80 connected the Surrey village of Kingswood with central London, either via the Northern Line extension to Morden or, for the previous eight years, through running direct to Charing Cross. The London link was severed in 1982, when the service was cut back to Belmont and the southern section covered by London Country Route 422. This view at Rookery Way, Lower Kingswood, dates from summer 1969, shortly after OPO RFs replaced RTs on this service and the terminus was resited. *Roy Hobbs*

Borrowed Time

Below left: A downturn in Green Line patronage coupled with the introduction of new vehicles (RCs and Routemaster coaches) rendered several RFs redundant in the mid-1960s. Eight RFs, Nos 290-297, were loaned to BEA in August 1965 for the new Executive Express services linking the West London Air Terminal to the apron at Heathrow, pending the delivery of eight AEC Reliance coaches. Help from LT was again needed the following year, as this view taken in November 1966 illustrates. RF86 was subsequently returned to LT service, and was withdrawn by London Country in August 1971. *Mike Harries*

Rest In Peace

Right: The programmed withdrawal of the Leyland RTLs was well underway when RTL521 was caught relaxing in the pleasant surroundings of Clapton garage yard on 21 August 1966. Clapton became the last all-RTL garage, eventually losing the type in November 1967. *Gerald Mead*

Special Guy

Above: The GS class was designed for use on country routes with narrow lanes and few passengers. Not surprisingly, these services became obvious targets for abandonment over the years and 10 GS vehicles were withdrawn as early as 1960. GS29, photographed at Hertford on 16 September 1961, lasted until 1965. *Hugh Ramsey*

Passing the Pigeons

Right: Cricklewood's RTL1586 negotiates Trafalgar Square in November 1967. By the end of the year, only 229 of the original class of 1,631 remained. Route 60 lost its RTLs on 7 September 1968 when the service was withdrawn. *Vernon Murphy*

A Room with a View

Left: Box Hill and the late-lamented Dorking (North) station building, as seen from the photographer's bedroom. RT986 and RF217 enhance this unique scene, dating from April 1968. *Mike Harries*

Rushing to the Races

Below: Competing with Country Area Route 406F, which carried punters the two miles or so from Epsom station to the Downs, was the Central Area Express link from the more distant Morden Underground station. In summer 1967, Merton's RT2623 turns into Great Tattenhams at a junction which is now a crossroads, near the Asda superstore at Burgh Heath. *Roy Hobbs*

Double Killing

Left: The Routemaster was built to replace the trolleybus and, after that, the RT. Both objectives were achieved simultaneously in the case of former RT-operated Route 131, which was extended on 9 May 1962 from Kingston to Wimbledon to cover trolleybus service 604. Seven days on, RM1202, displaying its short-lived offside route number box, travels along Walton Road, East Molesey. *Geoff Rixon*

Damp December

Above: Winter coats and head scarves are the order of the day as RF584 picks up Christmas shoppers in the dreary surroundings of Onslow Street bus station, Guildford, in 1965. *Robin Hannay Collection*

21

Leyland Thoroughbred

Above: In contrast with the RTs and RTLs, the 8ft-wide RTWs had bodies and chassis from the same manufacturer. RTW26 passes through Tooting in April 1966, one month before the class was withdrawn from passenger service. *Maurice Bateman*

Fifties Feel

Right: Although this view dates from 4 May 1963, the upper case lettering on the blind, the Northfleet garage stencil plate and the deserted surroundings of King's Farm Estate, Gravesend, convey the impression of an earlier era. RT621 originally entered service in August 1948, but with a roofbox body. *Gerald Mead*

23

Hail and Farewell

Left and right: The final trolleybus conversion stage included the original London United Tramways network, and it was only fitting, therefore, that trolleybus No 1 ('The Diddler') should be exhumed from Clapham Museum for the commemorative run on the last day, 8 May 1962. Here we see No 1 in Stanley Road, Fulwell; remarkably, the conductor on the platform is Mr Ron Hadland, who had performed this duty on the first day, 16 May 1931.

The second trolleybus on the commemorative run was L3 class No 1521, also seen in Stanley Road. This vehicle was subsequently saved through the generosity of Cohen's, the scrap merchant, and now lives at Carlton Colville near Lowestoft. *Geoff Rixon*

Pole Position

There is a proliferation of vertical columns in this May 1969 shot of RT300 entering Golders Green bus station. Of particular interest are the two dark green posts which used to support trolleybus wires, and owed their continuing existence to the fact that street lights were attached to them.
Dave Brown

No Clutter

In contrast with RT300's environment, RT4758 experiences the
aesthetic charms of Farningham on its journey from Sevenoaks in July
1969. However, this is but a temporary respite, because urban
landscapes beckon further along the route. *Dave Brown*

Brand-New

Left: The entry into service on 18 April 1966 of the first six XMS Merlin single-deckers marked a revolution in London bus operation as well as inaugurating a highly successful marketing name, Red Arrow, which lives on today. Taking advantage of relaxations in the permitted length of buses, the XMS class had 36ft-long Strachans bodies accommodating a mere 25 seated passengers and no fewer than 48 standing passengers. XMS4, seen here at Victoria station in November 1966, had a particularly interesting career, being the sole Merlin to receive a full overhaul and ending up with London Country following an exchange with XMB15 (see page 37). *Robin Hannay Collection*

Spare Wheels

Below left: Intended only as a temporary reserve following delivery of the BEA Routemasters in 1966/7 which replaced the 65 8ft-wide Regal IV 1½-deckers, MLL 740 achieved a remarkable life extension of six years, long enough to secure its preservation. Photographed at Heathrow in June 1968 and looking remarkably smart in its obsolete grey colours, the vehicle received the new salmon pink livery in the following year. *Author*

Worse for Wear

Right: This unhappy pair of country buses were lying at Aldenham Works in July 1969. The radiator badge on the GS seems to have come from an RTL or RTW. *Mike Harries*

Park and Ride

Below: RF568 reaches the top of the hill in Park Lane East, by the entrance to Reigate Park, on a fine winter's day in February 1967. *Roy Hobbs*

Flying the Flag

Right: Here, on 20 August 1966 in Romford, is the most famous postwar RT, the rides bus which travelled 12,000 miles across the USA and Canada in 1952, requiring the fitting of distinctive roof ventilators. *Gerald Mead*

No Room at the Inn

This view of RF480, Saunders RT4660 and RM255, taken in October 1966, shows the familiar tightly-packed line-up of buses parked outside the mock-Tudor Royal Forest Hotel at Chingford. However, within two years there was plenty of space, as this terminus was abandoned in favour of Chingford station. *Robin Hannay Collection*

Strange Happenings

RTL319 and RT2591 emerge from Hainault Street into Ilford High Road on 30 June 1962. Normally, this traffic would be on Cranbrook Road, but diversions and temporary traffic lights were in operation on this occasion. *Trevor Saunders*

Baffled

Left: An unsuccessful soundproofing exercise was carried out on RM738, seen here at Flamstead End on 9 September 1966. The modifications achieved only minimal noise reduction, but adversely affected the cooling system, increased maintenance costs and looked awful. The experiment ended after 2½ years. *Gerald Mead*

Visiting the Bosses

Above: Well-laden RT3725 pauses outside the headquarters of LT's Country Bus & Coach department at Reigate garage (Lesbourne Road) in summer 1967. In the background stands the original Bell Street garage of the East Surrey Traction Company which opened in 1912. *Roy Hobbs*

Down but Not Out

Left: Despite being displaced at Willesden by RMs on 1 September 1965, shortly after this photograph was taken at Victoria, RTW493 was still active on the last day of RTW passenger service at Brixton on 14 May 1966. *John Aldridge*

Third Time Lucky

Below: Staff opposition to the entry into service of the Country Area Merlins, XMB1-9, caused all but XMB1 to be converted into Red Arrows XMS7-14, with the exception being renumbered XMB15. Due to operate first at Addlestone in May 1966, then to be launched at St Albans in December 1967, XMB15 eventually entered service at Tring where it was photographed on 21 February 1969. By then it was on its third registration, having previously been allotted JLA 57D and NHX 15E. *John Aldridge*

Following my Leader

Above: After the demise of the trolleybus, LT's flagship RM class began sweeping away the RTs. One of the first services to be converted was Route 37, operated by Putney and Stockwell garages, the changeover taking place in December 1962. In June 1964, RM1345 precedes RT1524 across Richmond Bridge. *Mike Harries*

Overshadowed

Right: The last day of trolleybus operation on 8 May 1962 was dominated by events associated with Fulwell depot, doubtless because that was the birthplace of services back in 1931 and also home to six of the last seven routes. Not to be forgotten, however, was little Isleworth depot, which held its own 'last run' on the final evening. Prewar K1 class No 1117 stands at Hounslow before heading off for Shepherds Bush, reminding us of the well-kept condition of the Isleworth fleet. *Gerald Mead*

Taking a Chance

Left: As this summer 1966 view of Saunders-bodied RT1249 in Powys Lane, Southgate, was not the photographer's last shot, it is safe to assume that he was not standing in the road but travelling in a car. So who was steering? *Dave Brown*

No More Tourists

Right: The first 25 RFs, dating from 1951, differed from the remaining 675 by having glass roof panels and being 2ft 6in shorter. Mainly through the Private Hire fleet being disbanded, 14 of the batch were made redundant in 1963 and Premier Travel of Cambridge bought several, including RF9. This view, taken in Cambridge on 13 June 1967, shows the vehicle serving a different clientele. *John Aldridge*

Hire and Fire

Right: The 15 RFW touring coaches with their distinctive 8ft-wide Eastern Coach Works bodies were used exclusively on private hires and conducted tours until made redundant at the end of summer 1964 when LT outsourced these activities. Most of the class were exported to Sri Lanka but RFWs 1 and 6 merely crossed the river to St Thomas's Hospital at Waterloo, where they were photographed on 6 July 1967. Apart from wearing a different shade of green, both vehicles are still in LT livery. *John Aldridge*

Bay Window

Left: As part of the natural development of the Routemaster, LT ordered a trial batch of 24 extended buses, just under 2ft 6in longer than the standard 27ft 6in version. This was achieved by adding an extra half-length bay and small centre window, increasing the passenger capacity from 64 to 72. The inaugural service was Finchley's Route 104, on which the first 15 buses commenced operations on 8 November 1961. Here is RML892 at Moorgate on 14 August 1966, looking resplendent after its first overhaul. *Gerald Mead*

Green Scene

Below: This view taken in May 1969 at the foot of Box Hill epitomises LT's country bus operations which were about to cease after 36 years. RT4508 is some three miles out of Dorking on its long journey back home to Chelsham where, nine years later, the last green RT retired from passenger service, ending 30 years of country RT operation. *Mike Harries*

Sunday Special

Above: RT3233 operates the once-a-week 205A route through Epping Forest in August 1969, still carrying obsolete upper case lettered blinds. British Motor Corporation (Austin/Morris) cars figure prominently in this view. The 205 group of routes was withdrawn in April 1976. *Dave Brown*

Favoured Garage

Right: This view of RML2349 at Bromley serves as a reminder that Godstone was the first garage to receive Country Area RMLs in 1965 and, incidentally, the first to receive the Daimler Fleetline AF class in 1972 as RML replacements. Until the mid-1960s, Route 410 was reliant upon lowbridge double-deckers — latterly RLHs and, before that, the celebrated Godstone STLs — but then the road under the offending obstacle at Oxted was lowered to accept normal-height vehicles. *Dave Brown*

Last Orders

Below: RTL1338's visits to the pub at Sudbury would soon be over, although this smart vehicle was one of 13 to remain in service at Willesden garage right up to the last day of RTL operation, 29 November 1968. Some six months earlier, RTL1338 has pulled alongside RM2106 at London Bridge station. *Maurice Bateman*

Rare Outing

Right: Mobile Instruction Unit No 1037J, running on trade plate 403 GH, takes to the streets near its home base of Wood Green garage on 21 July 1967. The body is none other than that originally belonging to RT1 and has clearly had a recent repaint. An indication of how the vehicle deteriorated over the ensuing 12 years can be seen on page 73 of the earlier volume, *Heyday of the London Bus — 2.* Luckily, this historic bus was saved and is currently undergoing a major rebuild. *John Aldridge*

Doom and Gloom

The so-called prewar RTs, which entered service between January 1940 and January 1942, spent their last years on training duties before being replaced by surplus RTLs in the early 1960s. This desolate scene is at Clapham and depicts RT127 on 8 April 1962 nearing the end of its days, like the building behind. The bus has been fitted with unusual quarter-drop upstairs front windows. *Trevor Saunders*

Outcast

Eighteen RTLs were repainted green in late 1959 for Country Area use, but it was not until July 1960 that they were allowed to enter service. Disliked by drivers and engineering staff, they lasted barely a year, becoming the first RTLs to join the training fleet. This view shows RTL1275 at Welwyn Garden City. *Gerald Mead*

T Break

The reign of the illustrious T class AEC Regal single-deckers was about to end after 33 years with the withdrawal of the Mann Egerton-bodied country batch. One of the last survivors, T790, only 13 years old, stands at Tring garage on 26 February 1961. *Trevor Saunders*

Tired Tigers

The TD class of Leyland Tiger PS1s was introduced in 1946 and numbered 131 members. This view taken at Edgware on 5 May 1962 depicts TDs 121 and 99 showing their age. Edgware's Route 240A was the ultimate TD-operated service, lasting until 9 October 1962. *Trevor Saunders*

No Climbers

Above: Seemingly devoid of a staircase RT4718 crosses Hampton Court Bridge in April 1962. The offside route stencil plate was to vanish on red buses between August 1962 and March 1963, having fallen into disuse on country buses almost from the outset of RT operation. Indeed, the uncertainty over retaining of the plates resulted in the first 114 postwar RTs being built without them and a start made on panelling them over on the prewar RTs. *Geoff Rixon*

Fluctuating Fortunes

Right: No fewer than 175 RFs were strikingly modernised in 1966/7 for continued Green Line service and yet within a couple of years some were demoted to buses as the coach services suffered a decline in passengers. The relegated vehicles lost their pale green relief in favour of yellow and carried a different bullseye transfer. RFs 127 and 83 illustrate the contrasting styles at Reigate in March 1969; ironically, the bus is back on coach duty. *Roy Hobbs*

51

Awaiting Reshaping

Below: Not a reference to this RTL's eventual fate but to the programme of major restructuring of routes and extension of OPO working which started on 7 September 1968. On this date 177 new Merlins, mostly emerging from store, were inflicted on an unsuspecting population and many RT and RTL services were affected. This included Route 25, shared by Bow and West Ham garages, which saw its RTLs disappear, albeit in favour of RTs rather than Merlins. In happier times, RTL392 negotiates Hyde Park Corner, heading for Victoria. *Vernon Murphy*

Dirty Work

Right: The country lanes between Watford and Windsor via the Chalfonts have left their mark on the bodywork of RT4553 as it passes through Gerrards Cross in the winter of 1968. From 15 February 1969, the mud would be sticking to Merlins (in more than one sense); on that date, MBs and MBSs took over several RT routes operated by Garston, Hemel Hempstead, St. Albans and Hatfield garages. *Vernon Murphy*

54

Shining Example

Left: Cricklewood-based RM1610 travels along the Edgware Road, Maida Vale fresh from its first overhaul. The offside route number box has been painted out, but not yet panelled over, and the cream relief band has turned to off-white. Yet the vehicle still retains its original radiator grille, bonnet-mounted roundel and air intake grilles. *Geoff Rixon*

Misnomer

Below: In an effort to update the traditional Green Line image, LT proudly presented, in a striking pale grey livery, the new RC class of 14 AEC Reliance coaches in 1965. However, it was soon evident that the vehicles could not live up to their name, because little reliance could be placed on their mechanical capabilities. Consequently, they lasted less than 10 years on coach duties. Here is RC5 at Heathrow in May 1969, looking remarkably traditional in Lincoln Green, complete with roofboards, rear wheel discs and garage stencil code. *Mike Harries*

PRIVATE
To hire a bus or coach
apply 55 Broadway SW1
ABBEY 5600 or any local garage

MXX 227

447 Eastwood Station
Woodhatch
Reigate Garage

MXX 29

Hidden Depths

Left: Reigate garage held many secrets over the years, including the LT collection of historic vehicles and a variety of red buses used for taking employees to Chiswick and Aldenham Works (a legacy from World War 2 when bus overhauls were transferred from Chiswick to Reigate and engineering staff moved to this part of Surrey). In this early 1967 shot, various RTs, RFs and a GS hide in the shadows while in the foreground stand RLH27, sometimes used on Route 447, and a red substitute, RF387. *Roy Hobbs*

Sign of the Times

Above: In the days when the motoring organisations erected their own road signs, RF499 waits outside St Albans garage on 23 May 1965 while covering a shortage of green RFs. *Maurice Bateman*

Remote Control

Below: Potters Bar's Route 242, which ran along the top edge of the Central Area bus map, was about as far from 55 Broadway as was possible. In summer 1966 RT4351 travels through the countryside at Northaw, the RTs lasting until 30 November 1968 when, not surprisingly, the service was converted to OPO. *Dave Brown*

Bringing up the Rear

Right: Just to show that RTs were also elegant from behind, this summer 1966 view at 'Ally Pally' depicts RT2142 on the only route to pass through Alexandra Park. The service was withdrawn on 7 September 1968 when the Reshaping Programme started. *Dave Brown*

Left: East Grinstead was among the garages providing vehicles to join the temporary fleet of RTs and RMLs used for the 406F shuttle service on Derby Day, 1967. Fully-loaded RT4750 has almost completed the slow uphill grind from Epsom station. *Roy Hobbs*

Extra Horsepower

No Punters

Right: By way of contrast, RLH69 is totally empty as it leaves Upminster station on 20 August 1966 working a route which was too far east to appear on the Central Area bus map. RLHs had taken over from TDs back in 1955 and were themselves replaced by OPO Swifts on 18 September 1970. *Gerald Mead*

Staying Power

RF operation on Route 219 extended through almost three full decades, ending on 31 March 1979 when Leyland Nationals took over. This view shows RF436 standing at the top of Weybridge station approach, before the terminus was resited on Heath Road. *Vernon Murphy*

So Long

Left: RF35 has only just started its lengthy trek to Luton via central London in pre-M25 days as it passes along the foot of Box Hill in April 1969. In January 1977, Route 714 was cut back to Victoria and new Route 707 took over the northern section. *Mike Harries*

Wolf in Sheep's Clothing

Left: This is Bell Street, Reigate, in June 1969, featuring innocuous-looking MBS437, with its standee accommodation well utilised. Little was it known that the Merlins and their successors, the shorter Swifts, would bring unprecedented standards of unreliability on a huge scale. *Mike Harries*

Euro Star

Above: On its excursions abroad with the Double Decker Club in the second half of the 1960s, Continental Pioneer's RTL1050 attracted considerable attention from local newspapers and TV, as well as from the indigenous population. In this view at Arras in August 1967, these French children have probably never seen a London bus before. *Author*

Hello Dolly

Left: Racing at Epsom Downs has caused the Tattenham Corner terminus of Route 164A to be moved higher up Great Tattenhams, hence the temporary 'dolly' portable bus stop visible through the lower-deck windows. The distinguishing feature of the Saunders RT body — the rearward position of the offside route stencil fixing — is clearly evident in this summer 1967 view. *Roy Hobbs*

Space Shuttle

Right: With only 37 seats, BEA's 4RF4 1½-deck coaches were becoming less able to handle the increases in passenger loadings arising from the introduction of larger aircraft. The answer was to suspend RML production temporarily while 65 forward-entrance short Routemasters were built to run with luggage trailers, thus increasing passenger capacity on the prestigious West London Air Terminal to Heathrow express service. In June 1969 BEA No 31 (later RMA48) was photographed entering the Central Terminal Area at Heathrow. *Mike Harries*

Red Between the Lines

Right: This row of country RTs at Leatherhead garage is infiltrated by Norbiton's RT4296 performing a reverse turn on arrival at the terminus of Route 65A from Ealing (Argyle Road). RT981, fourth from right, became the penultimate London Country RT to remain in passenger service, lasting until February 1978. Leatherhead garage was demolished to make way for office development in May 1999. *Roy Hobbs*

Approaching Sunset

Left: Four days before implementation of Stage 12 of the trolleybus replacement programme, No 1474 stands at New Southgate station on 4 November 1961. *Hugh Ramsey*

Sharing the Spoils

Right: At its peak, buses for the lengthy 408 service from Warlingham to Guildford via Croydon came from three garages: Guildford, Leatherhead and Chelsham. This June 1969 view depicts RT2246 in Guildford; 30 years later, Route 479 took over the Leatherhead to Guildford section and the remnant of route 408 is now operated by Epsom Coaches. This renowned company has been in business for 80 years. *Dave Brown*

Rail Link

RT2420 stands at Staines West station, when the building was in its second incarnation, having started life as a dwelling and serving today as offices. The branch line from West Drayton was closed in 1965. Route 90 operated from the now-demolished Twickenham garage, which was tucked away near Richmond Bridge. *John May*

Unfulfilled Potential

The 43 members of the RCL class of 30ft-long Routemaster coaches were magnificent machines, but, by the time they arrived in June 1965, crew operation was rapidly becoming uneconomic on Green Line services. Here we see brand-new RCLs 2219 and 2231 outside Romford garage. *Maurice Bateman*

Cheap and Cheerful

Above: RT3422 was one of several members of the class to receive cream-coloured fleetnames instead of gold during overhaul in 1966, an experiment which was quickly abandoned. This rural view is near Essendon Mill in winter 1968/9. *Dave Brown*

One for the Road

Right: Carrying the familiar Black & White whisky advertisement which had adorned London buses for many years, RTW48, in the hands of a learner driver, has the road to itself at Marble Arch on a hot day in August 1965. By this time, many RTWs were in use as trainers to prepare recruits for driving Routemasters which, at 8ft, were the same width. *Geoff Rixon*

Eyesight Test

Below: In the later 1960s, RFs on Country Area routes were fitted with various styles of blind, including this version with minute via points, large route number and no prominent terminus shown. Pristine RF438, on loan from the Central Area, climbs Bell Street, Reigate, in summer 1967. *Roy Hobbs*

Souvenir of London

Right: Turning at Wrotham in June 1969, Swanley's RT599 is sporting a reconditioned radiator which, judging by the badge, was previously on a Central Area bus. RT599 was the third green RT to be built, entering service at Tring on 21 July 1948 with a roofbox Weymann body. RTs were displaced on Route 423 by OPO Swifts on 1 July 1971. *Dave Brown*

Last Hideout

Above: Noteworthy for carrying Guy Motors' trademark Red Indian mascot, the 84-strong GS class had shrunk to two when the last survivors were withdrawn at Garston garage on 30 March 1972. Three years earlier, GS17 and GS33 stand in the garage forecourt. *Vernon Murphy*

Going West

Right: RTL1549 heads into the winter setting sun at Trafalgar Square in November 1967, 12 months before the last of the Leyland 'RT's were withdrawn from passenger service. *Vernon Murphy*

Box Clever

Below: Following the decision in the early 1960s to phase out all the Leylands before concentrating on the RTs, it made sense to transfer older RT bodies on to RTL chassis at their final overhaul. Thus 23 RTLs were to receive roofbox RT10 bodies in 1964, including RTL1438, pictured alongside newly-repainted RTL1528 at Camberwell garage in winter 1965/6. *Robin Hannay Collection*

Routemasters Forever

Right: RMs entered service on Route 23 on 11 November 1959. Over 40 years later, this service is still Routemaster-operated, with RMLs and an open-top RMC (1510) operating with First CentreWest out of Westbourne Park garage. RM112 waits at Becontree Heath on 20 August 1966. *Gerald Mead*

Index of Locations Illustrated